Library of Congress Cataloging in Publication Data   Gantz, David.   Captain Swifty counts to fifty.
Summary: Captain Swifty and his animal friends count to fifty. [1. Counting. 2. Animals—Fiction] I. Title   PZ7.G1535Cap   [E]   AACR2
ISBN: 0-385-17527-2   Library of Congress Catalog Card Number 81-43239

Doubleday & Company, Inc., Garden City, New York

2 two

If Moxy gives one bottle of ketchup to Calico Cat, how many does Moxy have left?

3 three

Calico Cat is fishing for his supper.

Three birds on Calico's fishing pole.

4
four

While out for his morning spin,
Squawk spots something most unusual.

5 five

Moxy is diving for lost treasure.

We're five birds resting on our trip south.

Five pieces of gold.

Five eels in a treasure chest.

A school of five fishes.

I'm fifth

Captain Swifty is having a
nightmare. He sees six
little monsters in his dream.

Seven hats blowing
in the wind.

8 eight

The Captain is proud of his picture collection.

Count my pictures -
1, 2, 3, 4,
5, 6, 7, 8.

I'm eighth.

9
nine

Moxy loves ketchup, and he collects ketchup bottles. He has eight bottles with ketchup in them and one where Genie Bear with the light brown hair lives.

Nine Ketchup bottles, count them—1, 2, 3, 4, 5, 6, 7, 8, 9.

Nine blackbirds.

Genie Bear has five bracelets on one arm and four on the other. How many bracelets does that make?

I'm ninth.

10
ten

When he is not at sea, this is where Captain Swifty lives.

Ten stepping stones on Captain Swifty's walk.

Captain Swifty

Captain Swifty has gathered his crew together for inspection.

Eleven puffs of smoke.

12
twelve

Captain Swifty takes his troop of twelve little seascouts on a nature walk.

Twelve ants going home after a busy day.

Twelve tree stumps.

Thirteen black cats walk across
the Captain's and Moxy's path on
a night filled with spooky things.

14
fourteen

Morris the mailman delivers the mail.

16
sixteen

It's story time. Captain Swifty and his friends love to sit by the fire and read in their spare time.

See if you can count sixteen books.

17
seventeen

Seventeen mushrooms. Moxy is out picking mushrooms for the evening meal, and is amazed by the variety of sizes, shapes, and colors that they come in.

18
eighteen

While on his rounds, Morris the mailman rests at Peter's Pickle Works and enjoys a snack of his favorite food. Count the pickle jars.

19
nineteen

Nineteen clocks. Moxy is helping
Captain Swifty clean his
clock collection.

Thirty penguins meet Captain Swifty.

40
forty

Forty bees are chasing Genie Bear after he disturbed their beehive while looking for honey.

50 **fifty**

Fifty butterflies. Peter the pickleman's hobby is painting. When Beulah Butterfly agreed to pose for him, forty-nine of her friends decided to watch.